AMAZON INTERVIEW PREPARATION

A Step By Step Guide to Get the Skills, Preparation, Secrets and Success Tips to Win The Amazon Interview and Get the Job!

By

OLIVER MARTIN

professional before attempting any techniques outlined in this book.

By reading this document, the reader agrees that under no circumstances is the author responsible for any losses, direct or indirect, which are incurred as a result of the use of information contained within this document, including, but not limited to, — errors, omissions, or inaccuracies.

TABLE OF CONTENTS

INTRODUCTION

Any applicant who has experience undergoing interviews would be unsurprised to find out that all throughout the interview process, interviewers will be asking questions about their own company. After all, the interviewers want to know whether or not the applicant has had the due diligence to research the company beforehand, and they want to know if the applicant knows the direction the company is taking, and if they're compatible with it.

Whenever a prospective applicant studies a company, it's best to have a framework in place in order to be better organized, rather than reading haphazardly. The following outline can be used for researching on any company, not just Amazon.

1.   The Mission-Vision of the Company

2.   Corporate Culture and Values within the Company

3.   Main Products and Services

4.   Target Market

1. The Mission-Vision of the Company

Amazon's stated vision is: "To be Earth's most customer-centric company, where customers can find and discover anything they might want to buy online." This statement by Amazon demonstrates their goal of turning into the largest electronic commerce business globally. They focus on having a global reach, with excellent client service, with the largest possible product selection.

The mission of Amazon is stated as: "We strive to offer our customers the lowest possible prices, the best available selection, and the utmost convenience." Similarly to their vision statement, here they demonstrate their commitment to customer service and convenience. If we break down this statement, we see that they focus on lowering prices, while offering the best selection and convenience that they can to their clients.

2. Corporate Culture and Values within the Company

Amazon has a highly-developed corporate culture, with many aspects to it. It would be better for a prospective applicant to research online to discover the nuances to Amazon's corporate culture. There are many resources that one can use, foremost among them Amazon's website itself.

3. Main Products and Services

As we see in the mission-vision statement, Amazon's foremost business is as an e-commerce portal. However, Amazon is not a one-dimensional company, and also has other key businesses. It's relatively easy to search for the various businesses that they have expanded to, and it would be useful to research further to understand the teams behind each business, as this knowledge would be useful during the interview process.

4. Target Market

This particular portion should be nuanced to the product or service or business category that you are considering. In general, you should research the demographic of the customer that the group that you are applying for tends to target. The major data points that you should keep in mind when doing this research are:

1. Age

2. Income

3. Sex/Gender

4. Propensity to spend

5. Major Competitors

As an e-commerce business, and a successful one, Amazon has found a large amount of rivals and competitors. While they are too many to list, we can examine how Amazon stacks up against them.

CHAPTER 1

AMAZON'S SCREENING PROCESS

During Amazon's job interview and screening process, there are multiple steps to go through, usually composed of up to three initial screens then if qualified, an additional interview to be conducted on-site at the Amazon Campus.

1st Screening Stage: Initial Recruitment

The first screening step is not always undergone by everyone, but if ever a potential hire passes through this step, they will be talking to a recruiter who will give you a general overview of the position, then briefly inquire about your background and general interests. The recruiter will also predict which team would best suit you, and categorize you accordingly. Every now and then, if an applicant's resume is impressive enough, the recruiter will immediately connect the applicant to a hiring manager, skipping the initial screening stage. At the end of the day, the job of the recruiter is to filter the applicants and see whether or not it would be worth it for the applicant to be passed on to the second stage of the screening process. The entire process is often conducted on the phone; however, there are times wherein this process can be conducted by recruiter's face to face during career or job fairs at university campuses or other recruitment centers.

2nd Screening Stage: Initial Interview by Manager or Team Member

This stage of the screening process is to test your compatibility with the general principles of the company. The interviewer won't go in-depth when it comes to asking you about your technical and operational skills, but will mainly focus on asking you about their principles and how you would deal with situations, mostly using "Behavioral Questions". The interviewer may cover anywhere from two to four general principles during this stage of the process. This usually takes thirty to forty-five minutes, and similarly to the first stage, is often conducted through the phone, or during recruitment or career fairs.

3rd Screening Stage: Secondary Interview by Manager or Team Member

This particular screen may be similar to the second stage, or they may focus on other types of questions, but they usually refrain from discussing the applicant's technical or design skills this early, unless the role that the applicant is interviewing for is positioned in a highly technical working group. The most common types of questions asked at this stage are:

1. Scenario-type questions (Cases

2. Pricing Inquiries

3. On Strategies

4. On Vision

5. Tradeoffs

6. Estimation Questions

On-site (Face-to-face) Interview

If ever the applicant gets through Amazon's initial screening, the company will request for the applicant's appearance at their offices for physical interviews, and if needed, they will even fly them over. The physical interview process usually consists of about five stages of interviews, each being around forty-five minutes to an hour each. The questions asked often vary, and during one of the five interviews, you will come face to face with the manager or team member you spoke to over the phone. However, the most important interviewer that you will meet during this stage of the process is what they call the "Bar Raiser". This interviewer is a designated impartial employee, whose role is to ensure that the applicant belongs to the upper half of the candidates at that level. Naturally, this interview tends to be the most difficult one, and every applicant will be challenged during it. Making an impression on the bar raiser is quite important, as they have veto power, meaning that the second that they feel that you shouldn't proceed, no matter the opinions of the other interviewers, the applicant will end the process at that stage.

After passing through the various screening stages and the interview process, results are relatively quick. An applicant will be informed of the hiring team's decision about a week after the last set of interviews.

CHAPTER 2

STUDY & PREPARATION

"Proper preparation prevents poor performance."

When it comes to getting ready for an interview for a job position in a massive tech company like Amazon, you can never prepare too much.

As a company, Amazon values their candidates who put the time and effort to study and prepare for the interview.

We will speak about these principles in detail and how you should study and prepare to answer questions based on them later in this chapter.

According to David Anderson, Head of Technology, Amazon FreeTime—who has interviewed hundreds of candidates at Amazon over many years—Amazon does not believe in keeping what they look for in a potential candidate a secret. Since they have made their intentions public, they definitely expect their candidates to do their research and be prepared when they come for an interview.

It is important to understand that study and preparation to get a job at Amazon are not just about reading a few articles regarding the company history and the culture. You need to deeply study the Leadership Principles of Amazon, understand how you have leveraged them in your previous jobs, and prepare to answer simulation questions the interviewer will pose concerning potential scenarios you may face during your job at Amazon, and the successful decisions you will make based on them.

In order to effectively face an Amazon interview, you need to have a good understanding about the company and its culture, updated and functional knowledge about the particular industry, and a clear idea about what your job position entails.

Studying the Industry

Amazon prides itself on hiring the best people in the business.

You are required to have an updated and functional knowledge about the e-commerce industry, since all aspects of the company will ultimately be connected to the industry that it is a part of.

This is especially important for the candidates with positions which has allowed them to work across industries. If you do not have direct experience working for an e-commerce company, take time to fully understand the differences and the ways you will have to approach certain situations differently when fulfilling your responsibilities in the context of a data-driven e-commerce company.

Keeping a critical mind when you are studying the industry is also important. Rather than looking at all the positive aspects, look at what you feel to be negative and make sure you have a sound and thorough explanation about why you consider that aspect to be negative, if you were asked during the interview.

Understand that e-commerce is a fast-moving industry that requires constant updating of knowledge and skills. It requires innovation, diligence, and most of all the will to be flexible and change in order to have a successful career. E-commerce is an ever-growing industry that will only expand and be bigger with better opportunities in the future. Therefore, your efforts and energy will only be rewarded with time.

Studying the job Description and Your Unit

When you are seeking to score a job position in a company as massive and competitive as Amazon, you use every single small help you can get—especially if it is coming from the company itself.

Surprisingly, there are too many candidates who overlook or underutilize one of the most important pieces of information the company directly gives you—your job description.

There is a great wealth of knowledge that will definitely help you in the interview, from giving you talking points to understanding your strengths and weaknesses for this particular position. Read your job description thoroughly and note the specific phrases and statements that distinguish this position at Amazon when compared to other companies.

Studying a few job postings by Amazon will show you recurring phrases such as, "customer-focused," "data-driven," and "being peculiar." Understanding these small details and including them in your answer will be what distinguishes you from the rest of the many qualified candidates, who will probably give generic answers during the interview.

Most people approach the study and preparation for an interview by trying to find what kind of questions Amazon recruiters ask. A more effective way of expecting this is studying your job description and putting together answers based on what questions they might ask according to the details in the description. Brainstorm about what specific questions they might ask you. Preparing for generic questions recruiters may have asked others does usually give the best results.

CHAPTER 3

INTERVIEW PREPARATION

In many respects, this complete book is about preparing for a job interview. Every chapter has tips and strategies that can help you to be more prepared. Careful preparation can help you to overcome your nervousness in an interview, but even more important it can help you to be more successful.

The following provide some thoughts on preparing for an interview. Many of these thoughts are also repeated elsewhere in the book. Hopefully, their repetition will help you to better understand their importance in contributing to your interview success.

Interview time

It is critical to know the time, date and location of your interview. Based on this information you can set a schedule for reviewing the tips in this book as well as considering any other information that you might have to help you in the interview. I recommend that you visit the place of your interview a day or two before your interview so you have a good idea how long it takes you to get there. Plan on being fifteen minutes early on the day of your interview.

Research the company

Before you attend an interview; learn as much as you can about the company. You can do this by exploring the company website, by doing an internet search, through Facebook, Twitter, or even through news in your local newspaper. It would also be very helpful to talk to someone who already works for the company if you know such a person.

Being knowledgeable about a company's profile, its goals, its products and services, and its future plans can be invaluable to you in a job interview. Sometimes, interviewers even ask, "What do you know about our company?" Preparation can help you to excel in this answer. Even if you are not asked this question, you can still include company information in your answers to other questions.

When you demonstrate your knowledge about a company, you are showing your strong interest in working for that company. This kind of preparation can be the difference between having an excellent interview and an outstanding one.

Practice, practice, practice

Having worked at an employment center where we offered a wide range of workshops related to successfully getting hired, I found it remarkable that most job seekers said that their greatest fear was the job interview, yet the workshops we offered on job interviews had the poorest attendance. Attendance for resume writing workshops, or how to write a cover letter, were terrific. The same people who attended these workshops avoided the job interview workshop like the plague.

Having talked to many clients about their failure to attend the job interview workshop, the major reason given was that the workshop involved role-playing a job interview. Most people simply said this would be too nerve wracking for them to do. The same people also admitted their fear of real interviews.

If you want to be proficient in playing a musical instrument or in a sport, you need to practice. Success in a job interview is no different. You can read books and articles about how to achieve success in an interview, but unless you actually practice these tips, you will struggle to be successful in an interview.

Over and over again, I have seen people complete a workshop that involved role-playing a job interview and then go out and have a successful job interview.

Even if you don't have access to help from a local career center, you can still practice a job interview at home. Have a friend ask you the questions (even better if you have a friend that has actually been involved in interviewing people for jobs).

As each question is asked, answer the question as though you were in a real job interview. As most cell phones have a recording feature, film your interview and then review your results. Identify specific questions that you need to practice further, or work on any of your communication skills that might help you to be more effective (such as your eye contact or the level of your voice). For example, many people "trail off" their voice at the end of sentences without even realizing it. A confident person maintains a strong voice level throughout their entire response.

As you evaluate your sample interview, in addition to reviewing the content of your answers, ask yourself if you appear to be the kind of person who you would like to work with?

REREAD YOUR RESUME

A job interview often focuses on the content of your resume (and your cover letter and any other aspect of your job application). Resumes tend to be brief (1 or 2 pages). A job interview provides an opportunity for you to expand on what you have said about yourself on your resume.

As you read your resume, constantly ask yourself two questions. First, ask yourself to recall situations in a previous job where you accomplished things that actually prove what you said about yourself on your resume. For example, if you said you are a positive person, identify something you did in a former job that illustrates your positive nature. It is important for you to do this for every skill (whether a personal skill or a job related skill) you identified on your resume.

While this can certainly take some time to complete, your efforts will be well rewarded as this preparation will help you to better answer many of the interview questions that you are asked.

Reread the job advertisement

In the same manner that you reread your resume, do the same for the job advertisement (if there was no actual job advertisement, then do an internet search to find a description of what a person normally does in the job you are applying for).

As you identify the skills that the company is looking

for, once again identify accomplishments from a former job where you demonstrated each of these skills.

Your answers in a job interview will be much stronger when you back up whatever you say with specific examples from former jobs that illustrate whatever you are talking about.

Obtain reference letters

As part of your job search, you should ensure that you have a few reference letters (even one good one will do) from a former job, or from some volunteer work in your community (or a teacher/coach).

A strong reference letter can truly make a difference in applying for a job. By bringing a reference letter or two into a job interview, when you are asked about your strengths, or even "What would a former employer say about you?", you can confidently give your answer, and then add "Here is a letter of reference that I brought with me that supports what I have just said." Then you hand the interviewer the reference letter, pausing to give the person time to glance at it.

Sometimes reference letters can be hard to obtain. In some instances, you may have a copy of a job review or even copies of reports from former teachers. For some people, these kinds of references may be the best you can get.

Dress for success

How you are going to look is an important part of preparing for a job interview. is important as first impressions count.

I worked with one client who had ten different jobs in 10 years. While most of the time, this constant "job hopping" would be a strike against a person in applying for another job, the reality was that this person was good looking, had a great smile, was positive, and dressed for success (and he was charming in a conversation). The success that this person constantly had in job interviews was a clear demonstration that how you look can contribute to your interview success.

For those people reading this book who don't feel they are great looking, or who don't have big natural smiles, it is important to realize that the clothes you wear (and they don't have to be expensive) can make all the difference in the world. Dressing for success can help you to believe in yourself, and in the end your confidence can overcome your lack of looking like a movie star.

I might add that for some people you might actually have to subdue your appearance somewhat as I have seen some research that shows that overly attractive people (who look and act like movie stars) sometimes have trouble getting hired because there is a perception that it would be hard for such people to fit into the culture of the workplace.

Anyway, your appearance can definitely make a contribution to creating a positive impression in a job interview.

Organize yourself beforehand

Job interviews can be stressful. Rushing at the last minute on the day of an interview to decide what you are going to wear or to locate your resume can add to the stress that you might already be feeling. Having your clothes, your resume, some blank paper, any reference letters, a few pens, and any other materials that you might require for the interview ready the night before can lessen the stress you experience on the day of the interview.

As well, ask yourself whether there is any other documentation that you need to bring? For example, do you need a copy of any training certificates you have completed, college degrees or diplomas, copies of any awards you might have received, job evaluations, driver's license, Social Security number, and so on.

Why should we hire you?

Underlying everything that transpires in an interview is the question "Why should we hire you?" The key to answering it is understanding what the employer is looking for and then providing answers that directly related to the employer's needs.

Ask questions

Employers expect and respect people who ask intelligent questions in an interview. Examples will be provided in Although these questions generally occur at the end of an interview, they can often be more effective if they occur naturally during the interview.

For example, you might be asked "What responsibilities do you feel are part of this job?" After you answer the question, this would be a perfect opportunity to then ask, "Are there any other responsibilities that I didn't mention that you feel are part of the job?"

Another example might be when the interviewer says, "Tell me about a conflict you had with an employee in a former job, and how you handled this?" After you provide your answer, you might then ask "Do you have any company policies or guidelines that you would like employees to follow in a conflict situation?"

Write down a list of approximately ten questions

that you would like to ask the employer. If at all possible, ask some of these questions when appropriate during the interview.

During the interview, if you are asked a question that you really don't understand then it is quite acceptable to ask for further clarification. A very important part of any problem solving process is to ensure that you understand the problem before you seek a solution. Similarly in a job interview, it is important to understand each question before you provide an answer. If you are asked a broad question, you might ask for an example to illustrate the question which then gives you a better focus in answering it. Or, you can provide your own example and tailor your answer to a need that you know is important to the company.

Follow up

After every interview there are a few things that you should do. First of all, write down the questions you were asked and a brief overview of your answers. This information could be invaluable to you in future job interviews.

Secondly, write down a few things that you felt you did well in the interview, whether these were some of your stronger answers or whether it was even your calmness or confident manner. Congratulate yourself and celebrate the things that you did well. Focus on your strengths in the interview. Avoid "beating yourself up" over any mistakes you feel you made. Recognizing and building on your strengths can be an important part of being a successful person.

A handwritten simple thank you can enhance your impression to the interviewer. I have seen dozens of situations where an employer stated that it was the thank you letter that made the positive difference in a close race between two people. I have also seen situations where an employer kept the thank you letter (even when the job applicant was unsuccessful in getting the job) and then contacted this person for an interview when another job became available at the company.

In every aspect of the interviewing process, create a

positive impression of yourself. Failure to get the job you applied for may open another door if you leave the interviewer with the impression that you would be a valuable employee for the company to hire. Often there are several highly qualified people applying for a job. Being gracious when you do not get the position may open the door for another opportunity in the same company.

Little Known Ways To Answer Interview Questions

How to answer interview questions: Tips and Techniques

One of the most valuable things you can do during the interview is sound confident and knowledgeable when responding to the questions asked. Besides, how you answer questions, what you say when you respond, the details you provide, and the information you do not disclose are all paramount aspects of answering interview questions.

First Of All, Be Careful With The Information

You Give Out

There is such a thing as too much information, which should be avoided at all costs. Be discrete, especially when answering questions about your former employer or job. For instance, if you get into detail about how much you disliked your former boss and their company happens to be your prospective employer's biggest client, there is no way you are going to be hired with that big chip on your shoulder.

Know The Facts

It sounds like a no-brainer, but there are various cases in which candidates fail to remember details such as when they worked where. Show that you know your own résumé well. Do not act surprised when asked about something about your résumé.

Stay Calm And Take Your Time

Interviewing can be nerve-racking regardless of it being the first or the tenth interview you have attended. Stay calm and do not rush to give a response to an interview question. Taking time to organize your thoughts allows you to respond more effectively than jumping the gun and uttering something you later wish you had not said.

Answer The Questions Asked

While you should practice on the most common questions for interviews, be keen at the moment during the interview and respond to the exact question posed. Do not try to use your memorized answers at the wrong places, since it may put your authenticity to question. Also, speaking while the interviewer is still talking is a big turnoff.

Show The Recruiter Your Real Self

You should know that there is a fine line between what you think the employer wants you to say and who you actually are based on how you present yourself. Presenting only one part that you think is good comes out phony and one-dimensional. Also, showing the real side of yourself allows the employer to see if you fit well with the company culture. Usually there is not much you can do about the culture since it is something the employer will look for and think during the interview. However, showing the real you is paramount for success.

Show That You Are Fully Aware Of The Job That You Are Being Called To Interview About

While this advice may seem obvious, there are people who walk into an interview without knowing what the job entails, even though they applied for it. Showing that you understand the job gives the recruiter confidence that you are ready to take on the task.

Show That You Took Time To Learn About The Employer

After doing pre-interview company research, be sure to use that information in your conversation with the employer. This preparation shows that you are a meaningful resource to partake in the fulfillment of organizational goals.

Prove That You Have The Skills And

Personality For The Job

Remember to provide evidence that you really have the skills it takes to handle the job. Personality also determines if you are able to take on a job or not. If the job requires a lot of interactions, a shy person may not be suitable. On the other side, an extrovert might not be considered if the job is done within a cubicle office without much outside interaction. Your job experience and even the appropriate life stories help the recruiter see that you can manage to get things done without being pushed.

Show That You Have Reasonable Expectations

Beyond being good for the job, employers also want to know if the job will fit you well. An unhappy employee is not good for anyone, and no employer wants to experience high rates of turnover and go through the process of recruitment and training all too soon again. Do not portray too high or too low of expectations about the job for the employer to ensure that they can maintain you. Happiness breeds satisfaction, which in turn breeds productivity and reduces turnover.

Prove That You Are Resourceful

Most employers welcome employees who are seeking to find ways of improving things, such as better quality, more efficient processes, and cost-cutting mechanisms. They are not looking for someone who will just spin a lot of irrelevant ideas. Be sure to demonstrate your ability to initiate useful change.

Show That You Are Flexible/Adaptable

We are living in times when businesses need flexible and adaptable people, attributes which are especially useful for multinational corporations. The interviewer will most probably use behavioral questions about how you handled situations in the past to assess your ability to get used to a new environment. Be sure to sell that you would handle change well.

Show That You Are Not High Maintenance

Some of the mistakes interviewees make include getting into the interview room with frustration written all over their faces for something like having to wait for a while. Others call or email with a lot of questions ahead of time. Showing you expect too much sends a negative light of you to the recruiter.

Show That You Are A Problem Solver

During interview preparation, you may want to gather all the facts and ensure that the organization you are interviewing actually has a problem to solve by hiring you. In fact, it is good to approach the interview with the mentality that your presence in the organization will be helpful.

While you should employ your skills and experiences to show how you have been a good problem solver in the past, it is advisable to not act like the organization is faulty and that you are trying to fix it. If the question of how you would improve the company is posed, use facts and describe how you think your skills are a great asset.

Show That You Respect Management

Any employer wants to ascertain whether you are a person of character who treats their leaders with utmost courtesy. None of your responses should come off showing as if you are smarter than the leaders as this attitude does not play well. Do not try to put others down even if they are terrible.

CHAPTER 4

GETTING AN INTERVIEW INVITATION LIKE A TRUE PROFESSIONAL

So you've received an invitation for a job interview. You must be ecstatic! Or possessed with sheer fear. This is the point where you start doubting yourself. This is where your excited optimism starts to blend with panic so that you wouldn't know where one begins and the other ends. Relax. At this phase, your time becomes your most precious asset so don't waste it by focusing on your emotions. Instead, concentrate on how you could increase your chances of acing the interview by receiving the invitation like a true professional.

The first step would be to issue a prompt response. Before that, however, make sure that you've checked or re-checked your schedule for that day. Unless absolutely necessary, re-scheduling is a no-no. Employers are looking for people who are organized and dependable. They are unlikely to warm up to candidates who show little regard for their time and efforts.

When you receive the invitation by phone, receive it calmly and in a business-like tone, even when inside, you feel like yelling and jumping up and down. Make sure that your voice is loud and clear enough to be heard on the line. Think before you speak so you that you ensure that you use proper grammar. If your resume was well-written (and for an employer to call, it must have been), then he/she is expecting you to be well-spoken as well. To prove otherwise would be disappointing. Make sure that you talk in complete sentences and strive to avoid lengthy pauses.

Smile and stand upright. The latter provides you with confidence and this will be evident in your voice. While the person at the end of the line may not be able to see you, smiling over the phone will aid in adding a hint of natural warmth in your tone.

Important: The phone call may, in itself, be a form of a preliminary screening interview prior to a face-to-face interview. So manage your emotions and pay close attention to the questions that the caller is asking. Even when it's not an initial interview, treat it like one. Write down all of the information that the caller is giving you. Don't put the phone down until you have gathered the following pertinent data:

the name of the caller and his/her position/title in the company;

the company's name;

the date and time and the venue for the interview;

the name(s) of the interviewer(s);

the contact number(s) of the person(s) you will be meeting with on that day.

Don't hesitate to ask for directions. Here's a professional way of requesting them:

"I'm afraid I'm not very familiar with that area. Is it possible for you to tell me the best ways to get there from _____?"

One of the greatest mistakes that interviewees make is to show up late for interviews because they couldn't find the location. If possible, locate and visit the spot a day or days before the interview. This way, you can accurately calculate the amount of time needed to get there, get an idea of the traffic situation in the area, etc.

How should you end the conversation?

The smartest way would be to do it by repeating vital information to the caller. This way, he/she can correct any mistakes.

Example: "I'll be at (address of the venue) on (date of the interview) at (time of the interview) and look for (contact person(s) or interviewer)."

If you're already speaking with your future interviewer, then your closing statement should convey how you're looking forward to the meeting.

Example: "Very well, Mr./Ms./Mrs. _____, I shall look forward to meeting you at (address of the venue) on (date of the interview) at (time of the interview). Thank you so much for calling."

What if the interviewer/caller sets a schedule

and you're not sure if you're available on that date/time?

If you're anticipating a call from a potential employer, you should always have a calendar, a pen, and a paper on hand. If, somehow, you're still caught unprepared, then inform the caller that you will call again to confirm your availability on that date/time.

You need to make the return call as soon as possible. Also, when doing this, make sure that you provide a specific time which you, of course, must follow.

Example: "I need to consult my calendar. It's 9:30 a.m. now. Is it possible for me to call you back in half an hour, around 10 a.m. today?"

What if you're sure that you can't make it at the appointed time?

Then say so. Your unavailability does not warrant an explanation.

Wrong: "I'm sorry, but I can't have the interview on

Wednesday because I have to…"

Correct: "I'm afraid I won't be able to have the interview on Wednesday. Any time before or after that is fine with me."

Once you've both decided on a convenient date and time, try your best not to reschedule. That said, sometimes emergencies just come up. If you really, really need to reschedule an interview, then the best you can do is to minimize the damage by presenting your reason in the best possible light.

Example: In case of "professional emergencies," say something like:

"I sincerely apologize for any inconvenience this may cause you. However, I just cannot let the rest of my colleagues down."

You may have gained a negative point by getting the interviewer entangled in your scheduling conflict, but at least this statement gives evidence to your professional dedication and excellent moral character.

Receiving an Interview Invitation While At Work

What if you're looking for a new job without the knowledge of your current manager? What if the caller tries to contact you while you're at the workplace?

In such situations, any of the following responses may be appropriate:

"Can you give me a minute? I just need to close the door."

You don't have to explain why. You need only say that the conversation must be kept confidential. If the caller is just as professional as you are, then he won't pry. Don't mention that you're looking for job interviews behind your boss's back or that you're afraid your boss will fire you when he finds out you're looking for a new job. This communicates two things: disloyalty to your boss and fear of your current employer. Neither of these things will make you attractive to future employers.

What if you work in a cramped workspace where

you can practically hear your colleague-from-the-next-compartment's breathing?

In such cases, it would be alright to say:

"Can you give me a minute? Let me move to someplace more private."

"I'm sorry, Mr./Ms./Mrs. _____. I'm afraid I'm not in a position to speak about the issue right now. Will it be possible for me to call you back later at six o'clock this evening?"

Make it a point to call back within the day.

When expecting calls like these, you should already have a sound plan as to how and where you would receive the call (ex. in your parked car).

Important: If you're looking for job interviews while you're still employed, it would be best to practice discretion. Refrain from disclosing this sensitive information even to your closest colleagues. The knowledge that you're hunting for a new job may make you appear disloyal in the eyes of your current employer. If you end up not getting that target position after all, things could end up badly for you in your current workplace.

Scheduling the Interview

If the caller provides you with the freedom to schedule the interview, the best time would be before or around ten o'clock in the morning.

In a research study done by Frieder, Van Iddekinge, and Raymark (2015), it was established that the timing of an interview is a significant factor in how quickly the interviewer arrives at a decision about an interviewee. While dealing with the first few interviewees, the examiners have fewer information that they need to process.

This enables them to create a decision about the applicant's suitability more easily and more quickly. As they start interviewing more and more applicants, the amount of data that they need to recall and process and compare also increases, making decision-making more challenging. Thus, they are compelled to follow the heuristic method for judging the compatibility of the interviewees with the job position. This includes making use of educated guesses, stereotyping, and relying on one's intuition.

The 2015 study was carried out by analyzing data from hundreds of actual job interviews that took place at a university job fair. The bottom line: If you have your interview earlier in the morning, you'll be able to catch interviewers at a time when they are more alert and attentive.

As lunchtime approaches, examiners begin to feel distracted with other thoughts such as hunger, food cravings, errands to run at noon break, etc. Similarly, if you schedule your interview in the late afternoon, this is the time when the interviewer's energy level is at its lowest. For the same reasons, you also need to refrain from scheduling your interview during the seasons where the company is at its busiest. Again, this stresses the importance of conducting research about your target company, and that includes knowing its most eventful seasons.

How to Dress for the Interview

First impressions play a vital role in the selection process. Your potential employer's first impression of you is, to a large extent, based on your appearance and your clothes. At a formal interview, candidate who wears a tie, stockings, and a suit will make a better impression when compared to a person clad in jeans and T-shirt. Therefore, it is of the utmost importance that you choose the right attire for the interview. Your goal is not only to make a good impression, but also a fabulous and grand one.

Men's Attire for the Interview

Suit

•   Men who aspire to impress the interviewers and win the job must wear a suit for the interview. It should be a solid color such as navy, dark grey, or black.

•   The sleeves of the jacket should be long and reach the wrists. They should cover the entire arm from the shoulder to the wrists.

- The pants must be the right length. They should not be too short or too long.

- Tie and Shirt

- The shirt should be white. It should have long sleeves and should have buttons down the front.

- The sleeves of the shirt should touch the wrists.

- You should not turn and roll up the sleeves.

- See to it that the shirt fits you properly and is comfortable around the neck.

- Do not forget to wear one undershirt.

- Socks, Shoes, and Accessories

- Wear a belt that matches your shoes. The belt color should pair well with the color of your shoes.

- Choose a silk tie whose color matches the suit.

- Do not make the mistake of choosing a tie that has pictures or animal characters on it.

- Your socks should be dark and plain. Do not choose any fancy socks.

- The calves should be covered by the socks.

- Go for conservative, polished leather shoes.

- You should not wear sneakers, boots, or flip flops for an interview.

- Remove all of your jewelry. You should not wear earrings for such an occasion.

- Carry a briefcase or portfolio with you.

Hair, Tattoos, and Piercings

- Trim your beard and mustache neatly.

- Your hair should be groomed properly. Choose a professional hairstyle, not a fancy one.

- If you have long hair, pull it back. Do not have it hanging untidily on the forehead.

- Maintain a professional hair color. Choose natural colors, not unnatural ones.

- Use a limited amount of cologne or aftershave.

- Trim and clean your nails.

- Cover all of your visible tattoos.

- Body piercings should also not be visible.

Women's Attire for the Interview

Suit

- You can choose to wear a dark grey, navy, or black suit to the interview.

- Otherwise you can wear a skirt and blouse with a blazer. Never forget to wear a jacket.

- The skirt should be long enough to extend below your knees.

- Never choose attire that you would when you go to a nightclub.

- You should not wear dresses. If you do wear one, then make sure that it is accented with one jacket.

- Stay away from "loud" patterns such as zebra or leopard print.

- If there are pockets, pleats, or darts in your dress, they should lay flat.

Blouse

• Choose to wear a matching silk or cotton blouse.

• It is preferable to wear a light-colored blouse or a white one.

• Do not go for sleeveless or low-cut blouses.

Stockings, Shoes, and Accessories

• Choose conservative, neutral colored stockings.

• Wear low-heeled and comfortable shoes.

• Sneakers, sandals which are open-toed, and flip flops should not be worn for such an occasion.

• Try to wear minimum jewelry.

• Do not make the mistake of decorating your arms with plenty of bangles or bracelets or wearing dangling earrings.

• Instead of carrying a purse, you should take a briefcase or portfolio.

• Hair, Tattoos, and Piercings

- Your hair should be well-groomed, and your hairstyle should make you look professional.

- If you have long hair, pull it back. It should not be hanging on your forehead in a clumsy manner.

- Maintain a natural hair color. Do not dye your hair unnatural colors such as pink or blue.

- Use light makeup. Do not use a strong perfume.

- Your nails should be clean and neatly manicured.

- You can use a neutral color nail polish. Do not use bold colors.

- If you have any tattoos, cover them.

- Body piercings should not be visible except for ear piercings.

General Guidelines

- Do some research about the dress code of the company. Look at the photos of the workers on the company's social media pages so that you will know what employees wear in the office.

- Choose clothes that make you feel confident and comfortable.

- Avoid revealing types of clothing.

- Select your clothes according to the season and the climate.

- Get your outfit ready the night before the interview.

- You should not wear a cocktail dress, tuxedo, or sequins.

- You should tuck in your shirt. Your shirt should be clean, starched, and unwrinkled.

- You must avoid clothes that are tight or have gaping buttons.

- The pant's waist should sit on your natural waist.

- Do not wear shorts.

- Do not smoke on the day of your meeting with the employers.

- Be sure to brush your teeth properly. Make sure your breath is fresh.

- Do not eat candy or chew gum when you go for an interview.

The interview attire depends on the kind of job you have applied for. Your choice of an outfit is dependent on the company's dress code. It can be formal for an established organization, informal for an internship or a summer job, or casual for a start-up. Regardless of the company and the position you are seeking, remember that you should look refined and professional when you appear for an interview.

If your interview takes place in some informal environment, you can choose business casual attire. This is less formal than a suit, but at the same time, it is more refined than T-shirts, shorts, and a sundress. For example, you can wear a button down or polo shirt with khakis.

You must find out beforehand whether business casual dress is acceptable. If you are unsure, you can call someone at the office or the person who schedule the interview and ask for advice.

The importance of a cover letter

Now that we have looked at your résumé, let's look into how you can write a strong cover letter. Cover letters are just as important as résumés. They are often something that people dread writing because they know the cover letter must be written for every job that you apply to. However, if you have a good cover letter, your application can stand out from the surrounding people. A good cover letter could possibly be the reason you get an interview or even the reason you get a job. Let's look into cover letters and how you can write the best one.

First, let's learn about what cover letters are. A cover letter is simply a letter written to the hiring team in charge of filling the position that you are applying for. It is a letter that explains who you are in greater detail compared to what your résumé can show. It can explain your personal history as well as your skills and achievements. It is personalized to the job that you are applying for so it can show the employer how you would be the perfect fit for the job that they're looking to fill. It can show the employer that you have researched his company and that you have done the behind the scenes work that makes you worthy of an interview or even have a job. It is something that helps the hiring team get to know you personally before actually decide to meet you.

Next, let's look into what the hiring team does with cover letters. Typically, cover letters are only looked at or read after the hiring team decides they like your résumé. It is the next step in the process. If your cover letter is read, it means the company is interested in you and they want to get to know you better. The company likely uses cover letters as a way to get to know more applicants than they could interview in the time they have available. They then use the information that they learned from the cover letters to decide which of these applicants they would like to meet in person.

When should you write a cover letter? Just about any job would appreciate one. Even if it is not read, it will still be worth the effort in case it is. Especially if it is a cover letter that is not asked for, including one could make you stand out from the crowd.

Cover letters can be frustrating because they take time, but know that they are worth it. They truly do make you stand out.

So, how do you write a cover letter? When you begin to write your letter, start addressing the hiring manager by name. Many people start their cover letters with a phrase like "Dear Sir or Madam," and this is simply not personal at all. If you do the research, it is likely that you will find the name of the hiring manager at the company that you are applying to. Experts say even guessing the name of the hiring manager by looking at names of higher up employees on the company's website is better than addressing the letter to a nonspecific person. This is because when you take the time to research the name of the hiring manager, it shows you were interested in the job. It adds a personal touch, and it shows you are willing to go the extra mile to make yourself stand out. This proves you are dedicated to the company and that you are a hard worker.

Next, you should begin by talking about the company and why you want to work there. It is good to add the company name into this section of your cover letter. This is because it makes the cover letter feel more personalized and it shows you are interested in the specific company that you are applying for.

You will then want to explain your skills. You want to show that you have something to offer for the company. You can do this by providing a small glimpse into your background that has different information than your résumé.

It is also important when you are writing a cover letter that you are honest and real. You do not want to sound like you do not care. You want to show that you're interested. If your letter is sincere, it will likely stand out from the other applicants that write cover letters. You also do not want to put information like "I am your best candidate." This is because this phrase is too confident. You do not know the other people who are applying for the job, so you cannot possibly know this. You can say that you are a great fit and that you believe you can add a lot to the company, but you do not know that you are the "best" person who will apply to the job. This phrase may possibly be something that the hiring team does not want to hear.

Let's look into how to write a cover letter paragraph by paragraph. In the first paragraph, you will want to introduce yourself. You will then want to tell the company, while you call them by name, why you want to work for them. You can tell a little bit about your background and why it fits in with the opening position they are hiring for. You can also include a referral source in the section if you have one. This referral source could possibly be a personal contact or social connection like we talked about earlier in the book.

In the second paragraph, you will want to talk about what you can give to the company. To find this answer, research the company and figure out what they need. Mention the company's goals, opportunities, and accomplishments. This will show that you are interested in the company and that you are dedicated to learning about what they need. It will also show you have the things that they need.

This information will surely make you stand out from the crowd.

Paragraph three is a call to action. Tell the hiring team you would love to have the chance to meet them. Ask for an interview. Tell them that you will be following up, and when. Then make sure afterward that you actually follow up during this time frame so that they know you are serious.

After these three paragraphs, you could consider adding any additional information that you want the hiring team to know. You could add anything that is not on your résumé. You can include your passions and hobbies if they relate to the job. This is especially helpful if you are applying to a job that you have not worked in before. If your passions and hobbies are related to the field, it can be counted as experienced.

After you finish your cover letter, make sure to proofread it. Have a friend proofread it as well and consider getting it professionally edited if this is something available to you and your budget. You again want to make sure that there are no errors because this could make the hiring team disregard your cover letter and even your entire application altogether. Make sure that you do not use unprofessional reading like abbreviations, emojis, or words in all caps. You have to write professional and tasteful.

Now that we have looked into how to apply for jobs that have openings, let's look into how you can apply for a job at a location not hiring. This is a new subject for many people. Most people think they cannot apply for a job unless the company is hiring. However, if you want to work for a certain company, you can reach out to them and network with them before they have open positions. If you do this, they may keep you in mind for when an opening shows up. They also may create an opening for you if they like you enough.

To apply for a job that does not have an open position, try to find personal contacts or social connections that work in that location. Let these people know that you are interested in working for their company. You could also go to professional events to meet these people. You could even just call them and ask them to have lunch so that they have a chance to get to know you better. If you get to know the hiring managers or people who work high up in the company that you would love to work for, they can vouch for you when there is an opening. This process does not guarantee that you will get a job, but it does make the hiring team keep you in mind for when openings come up, or if you are lucky it could make them create an opening for you. It is not a guarantee but it is worth a try – especially if you are applying to a place that has your dream job.

CHAPTER 5

THINGS YOU SHOULD KNOW BEFORE INTERVIEW

It amazes me how many people get to the stage of interview knowing next to nothing about the organization they are hoping to work for, or the industry they are trying to move into. These days, 30 minutes spent on the internet can give you a pretty thorough overview of most organizations. Here are a few key bits of information I would expect any applicant who stands a chance of me hiring them to know.

1. What are the company's mission, vision and values? These days nearly all organizations have these, and usually share them openly on their websites, recruiting materials, etc. Don't just read and memorize them, but spend some time thinking about what they mean and how you could help the company to achieve them.

2. What does the company do? What is the main purpose of the company? What is their industry and sector? The way I like to frame this (and the way I often ask candidates about this in an interview) is, if you met up with some friends tonight and told them you'd just been offered a job at The Big Widget Company, how would you describe to your friends what The Big Widget Company does?

3. What does the specific department that you would be working in do? Similar to question 2, what is the main purpose of your future department? How would you describe the critical role your department plays in the company to your grandparents or other relatives?

4. What recent news and events have occurred? What has happened to the organization recently that you should know about? Have they opened a new store, hired a new CEO, lost a major contract or just won an award for being a fantastic employer?

5. What is it like to work for the organization? There are lots of ways to find out about life inside a company. You can look online and see how people rate the employer. Companies like glassdoor.com give star ratings (provided by users) for companies as well as a "would you recommend this company to a friend" score. You can also look at the information the organization provides, but as you would expect, this is usually a very biased source of information.

By far the best way to get a sense of what it is really like to work for a company is to talk to people who already work there. In today's interconnected world, it is pretty easy to find someone who knows someone who works at the organization you are considering. Sites like Facebook and LinkedIn make a search like this very easy. Aside from being a great way for you to find out about the organization, you will score lots of brownie points in an interview if you slip in that you've taken the time to speak to a few people who work at the company.

If you do choose to do this (and I highly recommend it), ask if you can speak to some of the employees and find out a bit more about the organization and the people you will be working with.

6. Who will be interviewing you? Knowing a bit about the person or people who are going to be interviewing you can be extremely helpful, especially for more senior positions. There are a number of reasons for this. Firstly, it gives you a sense of familiarity. If you haven't been able to meet the hiring manager before the interview, then the first time you meet them is when you walk through that door. However, if you've spent some time trying to find out a bit about this person, maybe you've seen their picture online, and know a bit about their history, when you finally meet them it gives you a sense that you know them already.

Secondly, by knowing something about the people interviewing you, it gives you a chance to find personal connections. Reading someone's biography on a website or LinkedIn profile can tell you a lot about a person's life, such as where they went to school (and therefore where they grew up), if they went to university (and if so where and what did they study), where they have worked, what their interests are, do they have children, etc. I believe that most people share at least one common interest with every other person, you just have to take the time to look for it. These connections can be very powerful. If you spot that both you and your interviewer went to the University of Middle Earth, when you're talking about your education, don't just say, "I got my undergraduate degree from the University of Middle Earth"; instead, add in that it was a great place to study or it was located in a fantastic town. This offers the interviewer (who, having read your application or CV, is already aware of the connection) the opportunity to mention that they too went to Middle Earth, at which point they might ask you where you lived or if a certain pub was still there. A connection is born.

7. What is your elevator pitch? You may have heard the term elevator pitch used in the context of people who are trying to start a new business or venture. The idea is that if you suddenly found yourself in a lift with your ideal investor or business partner, and you only had 60 seconds before the person reached their floor and departed, could you pitch your business idea to them, covering all the key bits of information, in that time. It isn't about speaking really quickly and trying to cram a 10-minute presentation into 60 seconds, it's about distilling all of the most important information and delivering it in a calm, logical way.

During my MBA we were taught to develop a "personal elevator pitch". Instead of selling a business idea or investment opportunity, the asset we were selling was ourselves. Initially we wrote down personal biographies, covering all of the information we thought a prospective recruiter would want to know about us, starting with education, moving through experience, skills and knowledge, touching on us as individuals and then ending with our ambitions. As you can imagine, for some people this biography ran across multiple pages. The next step was to turn the biography into a spoken sales pitch. Again, these could be quite lengthy. Then we would practice them over and over in front of the mirror, until our pitches were concise and had a conversational rhythm to them. The final step was to test them. This was done in a giant lecture theatre with about a hundred other MBA students. The best way to describe it is probably speed dating. You would find someone you didn't know, introduce yourself, give your 60-second pitch, and the other person would give you feedback on how you could improve it. Then it would be their turn to pitch to you. We did this over and over again, each time honing our pitches based on the feedback we received. By the end of the day, I think I had probably pitched to 50 people and could deliver my pitch in my sleep.

I would recommend that anyone who is in the process of looking for a job develop their own personal elevator pitch. I realize that not everyone has the luxury of a room full of willing participants to provide feedback on your pitch, but we all have friends and family, most of whom would spare a few minutes to listen to you and give you some pointers. The confidence that having a pre-prepared pitch, which you can adapt to any given situation, gives you is invaluable.

Internal Candidates

Many of the things we have talked about in the preceding pages make the assumption that you are applying for a job at an organization that you do not currently work at, and for the majority of people this will be the case. For those who are considering a move internally within their organization, please read on.

Hiring an internal candidate is often more complicated than hiring an outsider. This is because people make a number of assumptions and misjudgments about how the process differs for them as a result of being internal. It is easy to assume that the people on the interview panel know you, like you, and are familiar with your work, and therefore the interview is more of a box-ticking exercise than a "real interview". Unfortunately, these assumptions often lead to people performing poorly at interview, often resulting in them not getting the job. Below are some important points to consider as an internal candidate.

1.   When applying for a job you will be judged on your application, interview and references. This is a really important point to understand. Candidates often assume that the panel's prior knowledge of them is what they will be making their decision on, and thus don't put the effort into the recruitment process that external candidates do. While it is impossible to prevent your experience of someone from influencing your thinking, panel members have to make decisions based on the evidence presented to them during the recruitment process so that there is an even playing field for both external and internal candidates. Therefore, I would suggest preparing for an interview as if you were an external candidate, with the interviewers knowing nothing about you other than what you have told them in your application.

2.   Don't exaggerate. It is common knowledge that everyone stretches the truth a little bit during job interviews. People's previous experiences become broader, responsibilities become wider, budgets become bigger and results become more

impressive. For external candidates, it is easy to exaggerate a bit: as long as you don't go overboard, it is unlikely you will ever get found out. However, for internal candidates, this is a much riskier game. An exaggeration from an external candidate becomes a flat-out lie from an internal candidate, no matter how small. The price for being caught in a lie is much higher than the benefit you are likely to gain.

3.   Show enthusiasm. Another assumption internal candidate tend to make is that the panel already know that the applicant really wants the job. When an external candidate interviews for a job, they usually know very little about what the job will actually be like, and they focus their attention on the positive things they have seen in the job description and personal specification. Internal candidates tend to have a much better comprehension of the job, understanding both the positives and the negatives. As a result, internal candidates often seem flat in interviews when compared to the enthusiastic newcomer. It is

important that you make a conscious effort to show the panel how enthusiastic you are about the role.

4. Understand your reputation. As an internal candidate, one big advantage you do have is access to the people that will be interviewing you. During the recruitment process, you should take any opportunity you can to speak directly to these people about the role, their expectations and, if possible, what their thoughts on you are. It is often easiest done before you have actually applied for the job when you can ask to meet with someone and tell them that you are "considering" applying for the job and ask for their thoughts. At this stage in the process, they are far more likely to be open with you. This will help you to understand what your reputation within the organization is and if there are specific areas of perceived weakness you need to address during the interview.

5. Sell yourself and back up your claims with examples. Sometimes in interviews internal candidates don't get (or take) the same opportunity to sell themselves as other candidates. If one of the

standard questions is "give us an example of when you have been involved in implementing a new IT system" and everyone knows that last year the interviewee helped to install an important new payroll system, a candidate might be tempted to give a very short answer along the lines of "as I'm sure you're all aware, last year I led the implementation team for the new payroll system, which all went really well". Both the candidate and the panel make the assumption that they can fill in the blanks, and everyone moves on to the next question. However, this robs the candidate of the opportunity to make sure everyone understands what a challenge this was and how well they performed during the implementation. It is risky to assume that this is what all of the panel members are thinking, when in fact their memory of the implementation might be that on two occasions staff got paid late and they had to deal with the fallout.

6.   Remind the panel of the advantages of an internal candidate. There are a number of very obvious advantages to hiring internally. Because the

advantages are obvious, candidates often make the assumption that an interview panel will have already considered them, but it never hurts to make sure the panel are reminded of them. In your responses, look for opportunities to highlight advantages, for instance the fact that as you are internal, your notice period might be a lot shorter, and once you're in post, you wouldn't take three to six months to settle into the organization like other candidates might. Also try to remind the panel of the risks of hiring an unknown quantity rather than someone who is known and trusted within the organization. This is also a chance to highlight your loyalty to the company; you're someone who sees themselves working there for the long term, not someone who hops from job to job.

Much as it might seem painful at times, the best tactic is to simply play the role of an external candidate to avoid making any risky assumptions. Make sure your application, CV, cover letter and interview performance are all good enough to get you to the next stage on their own merit, and don't rely on people being aware of your reputation.

• There is some basic, but very important, information about the organization you are interviewing with that you should always know before stepping into the interview room. This includes high-level information about what the organization does, what its values are, and specific information about the area of the organization you will be working in. Most of this information is freely available on the internet and shouldn't take more than 30 minutes to find.

• You should also find out as much as you can about the people interviewing you. This will help you to feel a level of familiarity with the panel and may allow you to find a common connection with some of the panel members.

• Having a personal elevator pitch that you have written down, rehearsed and memorized will allow you to answer questions about yourself with confidence and clarity.

• Being an internal candidate has a number of

advantages and disadvantages. The best strategy is to prepare for an interview as if you were an external candidate and not make any assumptions about what the panel members know about you and your work.

CHAPTER 6

BRANDING

Positioning yourself as an ideal candidate

You walk into a store and look at a number of comparable products on the shelves. Then you reach for one.

Maybe it's a product you've used or heard about. Maybe the design catches your eye. Or the color. Or the slogan impresses you. You are now convinced that the product you selected, beyond all the others, will somehow make your life better.

So you decide to buy it.

But why that product as opposed to others that potentially would make your life as good as or even better than the product you chose?

Why did you make your specific choice? Probably branding. A message that convinced you consciously or subconsciously that the product you have selected will work well for you now and for the foreseeable future.

The same thought pattern prevails when you think of getting a new job. You need to define yourself, almost like a product, long before you can begin a job search campaign. Before you attempt to develop a resume. Certainly before you even contemplate an interview. Your goal is to have the company you like most reach for you, not others, and take you home.

How do you make that happen?

You start by looking at yourself critically.

Stand in front of a full length mirror and examine the person staring back at you. Do you like what you see or, if you were meeting you for the first time, is there something you would want to change? Then ask yourself some key questions:

- Who are you?

- What are your major strengths?

- What excites you?

- What makes you unique?

- What is it about you that should attract and hold someone's attention?

- What are you most passionate about?

- What overall message do you present?

If you need some help in focusing on these issues, and getting an objective assessment of how others see you, you might try taking a Myers Briggs personality test free, online or the fee-based Clifton StrengthsFinder. They might give you objective observations to build around.

Throughout this book you will continuously see the importance of clear, concise, correct, even compelling messages that are intended to win the favor of your targeted companies. Gaining a deeper understanding of who you really are will give you the start to establish a similar message (your personal brand) that you want others to see and appreciate.

It all starts with self-assessment. Knowing who you are and how you are perceived by others. Before you try to sell your skills and talents to others, you need to have figured out your personal brand, that person whose skills and experience you really want to project to the world.

Be totally honest with yourself. Are you happy with the way potential employers seem to perceive you? Not just physical image, but the total you. Demeanor. Attitude. Communication skill. Behavior under pressure. Ability to fit into their culture, whether it is "do it yesterday" or planning-oriented, as a positive influence and a steady contributor.

If you haven't already done so, you should join LinkedIn and become a member of whatever groups match your talents and interests. Be aware that recruiters and hiring managers almost always will scan your LinkedIn profile to get a sense of if and how you might fit their opening.

Reviewing honestly how well you did on previous interviews will help you position yourself better for the next time. Are you like thousands of others who come out of interviews and, when asked, say they did great? If they – or you --- did so great, why are you still here?

What did you miss? Or, from your standpoint, what did the interviewer miss? Why did they reach for someone else? Do some Monday morning quarterbacking to be sure the next interview does, in fact, go great.

When you look back at your career, do you build relationships? Have you been sufficiently aware of political undercurrents in your organization or do you tend to be easily surprised by what seem to be sudden changes? Do your colleagues enjoy being with you? Do they seek you out for advice or friendly chatter? Are they comfortable having a meal or a drink or travelling with you?

If they were asked for candid comments about you, what would they say? What does that tell you about how you present yourself and how you are perceived by others?

Assuming you're not shocked by your answers, figure out whether you just need a minor tweak or a major change to improve not only your image, but the confidence levels felt by your peers or the people below and above you. But don't just think about it. Do it!

When, not if, you move to a new job, you want to feel welcome and important. You won't get there without being totally honest with yourself. But, first, you need to impress one or more interviewers. What will you do next time to make that happen?

What makes you so special?

In sales and marketing there is a concept called the Unique Sales Proposition (USP). Advertisers use it all the time to differentiate the product they are promoting from other products. It needs to answer three basic questions:

•   What major benefit does this product (you) offer?

•   Is the benefit relevant enough to excite the buyer (the hiring manager)?

•   How is the benefit different and more special than what the competition offers?

Once you have established your USP, you need to be sure that the physical image you project is consistent with who you say you are. You need to display a confidence that helps an interviewer see you as a more valuable candidate than someone of similar skills and experience. Displaying confidence is a matter of how you express yourself in both body language and how and what you say.

Stop and think for a moment. What, if anything, is preventing you from being your most confident self? How do you fix that?

For most people, learning to communicate in a clear, concise and naturally animated way means hours of preparation. But, if you do it well, you will undoubtedly move ahead of most of your competitors to the top of a short list. This is where use of a recorder and a mirror can help you improve dramatically.

Your goal should be to convince whoever you meet, especially a hiring manager, that you are who and what you say you are. Someone who can come onboard and make his/her life better. Right now!

Let's look at the facts. You're a professional. You've had "x" years of experience. You have some, maybe many, accomplishments and a skill set you've developed and honed over the years. That's the basis for your brand and your own unique sales proposition.

Now, let's look at the rest of the package. From a business standpoint, how do you present yourself at work? Jacket and tie? Business casual? Jeans and sweatshirt? How are you most comfortable? And are you confident enough in yourself to adjust to a new environment and dress standard, up or down?

As you begin a job search your physical attire should match the image expected of someone with your level of professional experience. Suits and ties for men and business suits for women are most appropriate for interviews. If you find that the interviewer is dressed more casually, you can always ask if he/she minds if you remove your jacket.

How you dress appropriately for your own work environment may be very different from the way you need to present yourself for a job interview. If the environments are different, dress up or dress down, your interview may test your demeanor, ingenuity and flexibility, as well as your talents.

You're not Superman, I presume, so you can't just change in a phone booth. (Besides there are laws against improper exposure and hardly any phone booths left). So what do you do to avoid tipping off a current employer or a nosy rival and still show up on time, fully-composed for an interview, looking like you belong?

You need to find a way. A friend's apartment where you can stash a change of clothes? A hotel room if you can afford the expense? A bus or train terminal where you can store a small suitcase and change in a restroom before heading for your interview? Of course, remember, no matter how well the interview went, reverse that procedure before going back to your current job.

In addition to proper dress, consider these other aspects of image. Is your hair styled and neat? Are your clothes pressed? You don't have to look as though you just stepped out of a tailor shop, but you should not look like you have worn the same clothes for some days or, for that matter, slept in them.

If you're a guy, are you clean shaven or, if you have a beard, is it neatly trimmed? Have you found out in advance if the company you're interested in has any issue with facial hair? Are you using cologne sparingly? Do you convey an image of respect?

If you're a woman, to what extent do you use makeup? Do you go easy on eye makeup and lipstick? Is your perfume subtle or do you leave a scent wherever you've been? Some image consultants recommend not wearing any perfume and only minimal makeup to any interview. Do you wear styles, colors and lengths suitable and flattering to your body build, but still appropriate for the company? In short, do you project an executive (professional) appearance?

You look the part. Now what?

Now, let's look at another component of imaging:

physical contact. Is your posture erect, or slumping? You don't have to look military, but you do want to look healthy, alert and confident. Is your handshake firm or limp? Do you maintain eye contact? When you speak, do you enhance, or lessen, your image?

If you are going to present a document, have someone check your spelling and grammar. Use Spell Check often, at least for spelling. Do yourself a favor and ignore the grammar component, which is usually awful to the point of being illiterate. If English is not your first language, have someone with strong English skills check your writing for correct words and phrases. Be sure to use only words that you clearly understand and can pronounce easily.

Does your voice tend to be too loud or too soft? Find a level that allows for good conversation and ensures you can be heard clearly and distinctly. Don't make an interviewer strain to hear you or he may think you are too shy or too withdrawn for the job you are seeking. Don't overpower him with your voice or he may see you as rude, disruptive or just plain annoying.

Is your language appropriate to the circumstances or do you have to consciously curb local slang, sarcasm, or off-color phrases? If you like to use humor, is it appropriate for this situation, particularly for a one-time impression? If you're not good at telling jokes, no matter how appropriate, don't do it!

Now you need to critically examine yourself in perspective. Who are you? And how close are you to who you really wanted to be when you started to define your brand?

Once you are satisfied that all of your image components are in place, you are closer to your definition. This is probably your best chance to have others see you as you want to be seen. You need to be consistent in your whole demeanor -- literally the sum of your components.

When you meet for any business purpose, or even a social purpose, you want to be perceived as the total package. Attractive. Well put together. With a pleasant demeanor. And an aura of competence.

In an interview setting, being perceived as an executive or as executive material could easily result in your being short-listed for an important and desirable position. Sometimes even beyond the position you applied for. Depending, of course, on your ability to explain your unique sales proposition, supported by the consistency of your résumé and your appropriate responses to interview questions.

Now add to that sterling image

As you define, or brand, yourself, always look for ways in which your skills and accomplishments differ from those of competing candidates. What makes you unique and more desirable? How do you present yourself as the solver of critical problems, particularly those that your potential employer may be facing? The reliable, skilled professional who gets things done well and economically. And who makes it possible for those above him to sleep well at night?

Under most circumstances, virtually anybody with

appropriate training and reasonable experience can handle the technical aspects of a job. Given the chance, most probably can learn to manage a budget or do a satisfactory job of managing people or producing and distributing products. But not many exceed the norm. And those who achieve great, even unexpected, results are even rarer.

So, this brings us back to the Unique Sales Proposition. No bragging. None of this, "it couldn't have been done without me," stuff. If someone respectable says great things about you, that's a valuable credential. Said by you, it is irritatingly obnoxious.

Your Unique Sales Proposition in a job search sense should set you apart from everyone else competing for the job you want. Supported by fact and any kind of recognizable documentation, it shows the quality and consistency of your contributions. You can cite your own company's non-proprietary figures -- overall performance of your business unit or industry performance –compared to what you personally accomplished.

Focus on your results

If it is appropriate, show your accomplishments as a Team Leader or as a valuable team member.

- Did you inherit the team or choose it?

- What were your challenges?

- What actions did you take to overcome negatives or drags against success?

- And what superior results did you drive or help your team accomplish?

That promotes your ability to communicate and to lead. And pre-supposes clarity of thought, decision-making ability, calmness under pressure and your ability to meld styles and personalities into a team that works well together.

Your brand should be reflected clearly, but concisely, through a well-constructed resume that illustrates growth rates, changes in rates, real dollars saved or made, or precious time saved and used to improve some other effort.

Your brand and reputation go hand-in-hand. The

more you are observed as a confident, accomplished professional, the more your aura spreads. To superiors and peers, alike, to competitors inside and outside the company and to search professionals.

When they have the need, you want to be the package they reach for on the shelf. Whether you are the best in your chosen area is the opinion of the buyer. Could they find someone as good or better? Possibly. But if they believe the sum total of what you represent can resolve one or more of their significant problems, they will choose you.

CHAPTER 7

THE COMPANY

One of the worst ways that you can begin your interview is not knowing the company well enough. By knowing the company you are interviewing for inside and out, you are showing your deep interest. You care for the company and took time to study them. This pays huge dividends with the interviewer. One with no knowledge of the company will be sure to be put in the do-not-call pile. Here are some things you should study beforehand. This information should be easily-attainable on the company's website and/or via the Internet.

- Company History

- Company Leadership

- Recent Company News

- Key Competitors and Market Analysis

- An Inside Perspective

Company History

As with the foundation of any sort of analysis, it's always important to understand the history behind something. This helps to uncover why and how something originated, and why they are where they are now. Maybe the company saw a new niche or had a competitive advantage in an existing one. By analyzing a particular company's history, you are able to understand why they are where they are today. This is also important so that you understand how long the company has been around, whether they are new or have been around for decades. This will further help you recognize the type of position for which they are hiring. If they are a relatively new company, perhaps they are looking for someone for a particular position who will be able to handle many tasks and get the job done, while if they are a multinational company that has been around for a while they might be looking for someone to perform a specific task for a role they need filled. Here are some important notes to take down:

- Year founded

- Who the founder was

- Original purpose for founding

- Where the company started

- How they have grown

- Where they have expanded to

- Important milestones (went public, bankrupt, sold off)

- Forward-thinking notes (have they published a desire to expand or go international?)

Company Leadership

It is important to recognize the leaders of the company. These are the individuals who either founded the company and/or are the current executive management staff. These folks lead the company from the highest level and are responsible for the company's overall operations and strategic outlook. By researching who these people are and what they've done, you are able to get a feel for how they operate the company. This also gives you an opportunity to bring up this during an interview, and it may be an example of how you would use a line of normally uncomfortable questioning to your advantage.

Example:

Interviewer: Our Chief Executive Officer has led this company for quite some time and is a pretty well-known figure in the_____ industry. He is an inspirational leader to us from the top down.

You: Yes, I read that Mr. _____ (C.E.O. last name) has been the leader of this company for over 15 years. He has consistently led the company to over 10% growth for the past 8 years. I especially admired a time when the company was going through a tough situation during the recent recession and Mr. _____ took the time to address each and every question properly during their earnings called. I have found that many C.E.O. s try to avoid the most difficult questions, but Mr. _____ was completely honest and forthright.

Recent Company News

Key Competitors & Market Analysis

Researching the key competitors and the market in which the company operates is a key ingredient to knowing the company. By doing this, you can understand who the company competes against and different areas within the specific niche they operate. Interviewers love hearing what you know about the market of the company. This shows that you understand their business and what they do. You should fully understand their line of business and what is currently going on in the industry.

In-depth research enables you to understand the competitive landscape of the industry, which is particularly important. You should research where the company stands vs. where their competitors stand. There may be several corporations operating in a specific area, but each will focus on a specific expertise in that region. This can also relate to your position. For instance, the company that you are interviewing for may be the leader in a certain region in landscaping, but it is trying to branch into another area, such as one in which a competitor operates. By researching both the market and the area, you are well-versed on what the company is trying to do by branching out and what the challenges are (like key competitors) in that situation. You can really gain bonus points in this area and shock the interviewer by showcasing your knowledge. Let's take a look at how.

Example:

Interviewer: I am not sure how much you know about the position, but it is pretty new. We are trying to branch out into _____ and this position is vital for this type of growth.

You: Yes, I've researched the _____ market pretty thoroughly. I understand that {insert company name} has always been focused on _____ and the leader in the_____ area of the market, but their goal is to expand into the _____ part of the market. I know that competitors X and Y are the primary leaders in this area, but I think there are several areas for growth to be had. Competitor X has recently been losing market share in the area by their weakness in customer relationship management. I think using the strength of {insert company name}'s proven customer relationship strength will allow the company to gain market share in this area.

By using the information you researched, you are able to show you know the competitors, market, and most importantly, how you believe the company can grow in that area. This shows the interviewer that you understand where the company is, where it is going, and what is being done to achieve the goal.

An Inside Perspective

With information available so freely these days, it's quite easy to find ANYTHING on the Internet. A basic Google search for reviews on the company might yield more than you'd expect. Glassdoor.com has an "inside look at jobs & companies" and provides a place for past and current employees to review the company they work/worked for, and features thousands of companies. Contributors usually give an anonymous, truthful review of the company. In addition to this, you'll find salary expectations AND information about their interview processes. I urge you to do some research here, as it will give you an unbiased view on the company, their culture, and most importantly, the interview process. Who better to hear from than the folks who've both interviewed AND worked there?

The Position

Knowing It

When originally applying for the job, you should have come across a job description. This is the key to your interview preparation and should not be overlooked. The company spends a lot of time putting this description together in search of their desired candidate. It contains an overview of the company, the responsibilities of the position, and the desired/required qualifications and experience. If you were never provided with one prior to the interview, ask the company for one. In addition to this, you should talk with the hiring representative and ask them what qualifications are the MOST important for the position. This will allow you to focus more of your efforts on these traits.

If you study this well, you can tweak the way that you explain yourself during the interview toward what the company is looking for. Basically, you can tell them exactly what they want to hear. Let's take a look at an example:

- Project Manager XYZ Company

- Desired Qualifications: 1-3 Years of project management experience

- Excellent knowledge of Microsoft Excel

- Ability to navigate through unclear environments

- Ability to multitask

- Ability to work well with a team, as well as alone

More often than not, you will be asked to walk through your resume, which is where you can explain how you have accomplished each one of these qualifications, or at least refer to them.

Interviewer: Please walk me through your resume

You: Sure. My first job experience was as part of a ten-person team focused on selling a brand new product to the Southeast region of the country. Since the product was new, there was no proven road map to follow. Every member of the team had to take on several tasks in order to meet deadlines. From creating excel spreadsheets to analyzing our sales numbers to meeting with clients, we all had to roll up our sleeves and get the job done. What made this experience especially challenging was the fact that we were all located in different regions, but I learned a tremendous amount from it. We were all able to work extremely well with one another and this was proven in our sales numbers, which were double expectations.

This is just a simple example, and you would normally spread out your knowledge across all of your experiences, but do you see how we covered all of the desired qualifications? We didn't simply say: "I have 1-3 years of project management experience doing this and I know Microsoft Excel, etc...," but we tied these into our actual experience. This experience can be related to work, school, side projects, and so on. We were able to show our project management experience and multitasking abilities by meeting deadlines and tackling several different tasks for the role. We showed how we can work well with a team and alone by explaining how the team was scattered in different locations, but everyone still cooperated and got the job done. By offering this information, you are showing that you are working alone most of the time, yet are still capable of interacting with a team. Both your experience working with scattered team members and the work on the brand new product shows how you're capable of navigating through unclear times. I threw in the tidbit about Excel to show knowledge of Excel, but you can get more in-depth into it.

The interviewer will most likely ask several questions that are made up to see whether your qualifications match what they are looking for. By knowing these ahead of time, you can prepare accordingly and be able to answer these questions. THIS CAN'T BE STRESSED ENOUGH. STUDY THE POSITION DESCRIPTION.

Analysis Sheet

Once you've done all this research, you'll need a way to analyze the results. You can use your own or use the one provided (at the end of the book), but you should put together some sort of review sheet. With this sheet, you can compare and contrast what the company is looking for in the position vs. what you have to offer.

We will explain the outline format provided at the end of the book. The layout displays the responsibilities and requirements of the position. In the first column, you are expected to fill out all of the details that are given with the position description, as provided by the company, and in the second column, you fill out how you relate to them. In the third column, you will input how you compare to what the company is seeking.

The goal of the outline is to offer a snapshot of how

you compare against what the company is looking for. It allows you to focus on your strengths and deal with or be prepared for any weaknesses in terms of the position. This will allow for brainstorming ahead of time regarding certain areas that need improvement. For example, in the above outline, the position is calling for more experience than you have, so you would want to consider ways to compensate for that area. This might mean placing additional emphasis on your strong areas or mentioning how some other experiences make up for this lack of experience. Being able to see how you stack up at a high level is an essential part of preparing. Fill out the outline, making sure to be honest so you can avoid applying for jobs that you are not qualified to get upon interview.

CHAPTER 7

YOUR LOOK AND BODY LANGUAGE

In an interview situation, the way you look matters in the eyes of an interviewer. For better or for worse, we make an impression on the interviewer based on how we look. If we choose to make a sloppy impression, then that is what will remain in their minds. However, if we go all the way to have a better appearance, then we will make a strong first impression. It is important to maintain balance and to know what is right. It is difficult to get there at first glance. However, we must try to do our best in this way, and we can do a good job of this by minding what we wear, being concerned with our grooming, and managing our hairstyle, because these points will stand out inevitably during an interview.

What to wear

In general, most interviews will require you to wear

conservative clothing. In general, that includes a dress shirt, tie, and clean slacks for men and dress slacks and a blouse, a dress, or a blouse and skirt for women. It is important that you respect the rules for general appearance at the organization for which you want to work. If you see the people in an advertisement wearing a suit and tie, go right ahead and wear one too. It will help you stand out and show that you're really serious about the interview process.

For women, you should not wear anything that is too uncomfortable such as high heel shoes or other items. It is important to be as comfortable as possible. You don't want to look like you got off a plane and were sweating buckets due to wearing too many clothes. Instead, you want to look your best and as comfortable as possible.

For both genders, you should shy away from any kind of clothes that will draw too much attention to yourself. That includes flashy, retro, or bright-colored outfits, which would be viewed negatively at the interview. Remember that you are trying to make a strong impression, and it is best for you to stick with comfortable clothes that have earth tones or dark colors that will not make you stand out or look flushed.

Tattoos

One thing that many people wear these days are tattoos. They are becoming more and more acceptable. However, in workplaces, it is often best to cover them up rather than showing them off, especially if you work at a more conservative company where people would frown upon their presence. It is better to be safe than sorry. Tattoos can create a negative first impression when viewed by those people who have a prejudice against them.

Earrings and nose rings

Many people choose to wear earrings and nose rings. For women, a few not very noticeable earrings can be worn. However, nose rings are likely a no-no. A person should not wear nose rings to an interview no matter where you would go for it. For men, earrings could be worn. However, in many cases, you want to avoid those kinds of displays, especially while communicating with conservative bosses or managers who may frown upon them.

Grooming

For women, it would be expected that they should be well-groomed, and they should wear their hair in a way that is well-kempt. For men, they should be clean-shaven and have neat hair that is presentable. It is important to look your best for the interview and to present yourself as someone who has prepared their look for this day. In addition, you want to brush your teeth and floss the day of the interview so that there is nothing stuck in your teeth prior to walking into the room.

Bring a portfolio or folder with your briefcase

To appear professional, it would be helpful to bring a bag or briefcase with you and have your professional portfolio with your resume inside it. This way, you will exude an organized and hardworking attitude, which will help you score points with the interviewer.

Your look is an essential part of what you bring to the personal interview. If you mess it up, you will likely look like a slob and may not get a call-back or follow-up for another interview. Therefore, you have to do your part for the opportunity to come back to another interview or obtain the job. Don't think you can simply walk in with jeans and a t-shirt and land a job. It never works that way. You need to look your best. Put on your Sunday best, get out there, and make an amazing first impression. Remember that this may be the opportunity to make or break your candidacy. You can't mess it up. Don't go into the interview having not made your hair look nice or with wrinkles in your clothing. Do your best to get everything tailored and ironed so you can look stunning and dressed to impress. You have an interview, for goodness sake, so they must like you enough to bring you in. Now, break a leg and do the performance that could land you your dream job. Strut your stuff, enter the interview room, and do your thing.

Don't smoke before the interview

Another thing to realize is that cigarette smoke is something that can linger for a while, and when you smoke, you will find that you have the smell of cigarettes on your clothing and hands. The thing is, if you have smoked a few hours before the interview, then your interviewer will likely be able to smell it, and this does not provide them with a good first impression. Try your best not to smoke before an interview. It is crucial that you do this, because non-smokers can automatically notice if you have smoked or not beforehand. Often, the knowledge of the fact that you smoke can be a big turn-off to the people in the interview room, so it is best to hold off on the cigarettes before an interview.

Wear lightly scented cologne or perfume

If you want to wear something that doesn't smell too strong, then you can try using a few sprays of your favorite perfume or cologne, but you definitely don't want to overdo it, as that would hint that you're trying too hard to impress. Plus, it's just annoying to be wearing too much perfume, which can cause some allergens to flare up and cause you or your interviewer to sneeze, which just isn't a good situation all around.

Body Language Tips

It's your next big interview, and you're about to go into the room to meet HR or your potential supervisor. What should you do? Let's give you the rundown of the different things you can do with your body language, which can help you have a successful interview.

First things first, before you head into your interview, you have to prepare your body to go into the process. You will likely be waiting in a room before going in and the receptionist and potential colleagues may be watching your every move. It is best to get started immediately after you walk in. Stand up straight with your shoulders back and with your back in proper alignment. Remember that you are making a first impression and that counts.

You should put your bag on your left side to avoid the awkwardness of grabbing your stuff right as you get up to shake hands with the interviewer. When you get ready to go in, you want to be ready to move with everything you have. It is also better to bring less to the interview; obviously, don't bring a suitcase full of things with you.

Handshake

Give a firm handshake to your interviewer, though not one that is bone-crushing or limp like a fish. Simply give your interviewer a good handshake and make eye contact while doing it. This is important. You need to show both sincerity and integrity by making this the first gesture you have with the interviewer. This is important, because it is part of an American greeting and will help you establish a rapport with your interviewer from the beginning. Practice makes perfect. Nail it on the head when you do it.

Avoid crossing your legs

It is recommended that you don't cross your legs during the interview. It appears too casual and not professional. Plus, you might have to re-cross your legs in the middle of the interview, which could prove to be awkward. Therefore, you should keep your legs down and straight. Also make sure to face your interviewer directly.

Make eye contact consistently

It is important to make eye contact with your interviewer, but if you give too much of it constantly, then it can be threatening and rude. It is important that you maintain some eye contact to demonstrate that you know what you're talking about, but looking in other directions can also be helpful. You just need to know how to look at your interviewer with sincerity and interest. Looking away or not making eye contact could be viewed as a sign of dishonesty or that you're hiding something.

When sitting, have a straight back

When you are sitting in your chair, you should sit up with your back straight. Do not slump in the chair. Try to be comfortable while also projecting confidence. If you slouch or lean back in a chair, you might show that you are defensive and bored. Therefore, it is vital that you sit with excellent posture to make a good impression.

Avoid bad habits at the interview

Do you have some kind of nervous habit that you do at interviews? Like, for example, do you twirl your hair or twiddle your thumbs? Or, worse, do you sometimes bite your nails? You should avoid any of these habits during the interview process, as they will only reinforce the fact that you are nervous, and you don't want your interviewer to notice this.

Talk with your hands

Perhaps, you already naturally use your hands to talk and emphasize different points. Go right ahead and do that. Just don't do it in too much of an exaggerated way, because that would not be a good thing. It could mean that you're trying too hard during the interview.

Nod your head as you are listening to your interviewer

Next, you should nod your head as you are listening to your interviewer. It shows that you are attentive and listening to what he or she has to say. This is an important gesture in Western cultures and a sign of respect. Nod and grunt and say "uh-huh," a lot, and you're golden.

Lean in to show interest

You should try to lean in to show that you are interested in the other person and what he or she is saying; try to lean in and nod at the same time. This shows you're engaged and ready to go.

Case study #1: Keeping up the appearance

Jason went into the interview with a dynamite appearance. He had his best blazer on and had carefully crafted his hairstyle in the morning. He woke up at 6am to prepare his look, and he was ready to knock the socks off everybody in the interview room. He was pumped about the chance to make an impression and wanted to do everything to the best of his ability. Although he was a smoker, he chose to avoid smoking the night before his interview so as to not have the smell of cigarettes on him. He wore a light spray of his cologne, which everyone said smelled great.

As soon as he arrived, Jason sat up in his chair with his back straight against the seat. He shook hands with his interviewer and said, "Nice to meet you. Thank you so much for taking the time to interview me. I greatly appreciate it." Jason was ready to do his best during this interview. He nodded his head as he was listening to the interviewer ask him questions and talk about the job and the company. He never slouched and did not slump forward. As the interviewer approached a new question, he leaned in to give his opinion about a matter, which showed his vested interest in the company. Jason made consistent eye contact, but he never stared down his interviewer. Instead, he would look the interviewer in the face and a little around his eyes and would then look away as he was thinking of another response. This helped a great deal; the interviewer appreciated this gesture. He recognized that he was doing a great job. At the end of the interview, he shook hands with the interviewer and went out the door. He could feel that he had nailed the job interview and that he was going to get a call-back. Sure enough, he got the job. It all had to do with keeping up appearances. Clearly, Jason was on his best behavior for the interview, and he was rewarded for it. Go, Jason!

Case study #2: What not to do

Tim was a chain smoker. He would smoke about 40 cigarettes a day, and he was completely addicted to doing so. This was part of his nervous habit. Tim got the call for an interview at a company. He found a jacket and tie, but it was all wrinkled up. His interview was at 9:30am. Tim woke up late at 8:30am, and he had hardly any time to work on his appearance. His hair had not been washed and his mouth reeked of cigarettes. He rinsed with some mouthwash to make sure that no one would notice. Then, he arrived at the venue for the interview about five minutes late.

When he got there, he was shaking nervously. He desperately searched for a cigarette to go smoke out back. He was twiddling his thumbs. He got to the interview, where the office was a furnace. It was so warm because of the heating (it was winter, so it was cold outside). He had to take off his jacket, because he was sweating buckets, and the interviewer could see the stains on his shirt and could smell the stench of stale cigarettes on him. Though, Tim did have a good handshake and talked very naturally.

Throughout the interview, Tim would touch his face at times, and he was not very confident. The interviewer could see this. However, he was answering all the questions as best as he could. In the end, however, Tim felt defeated. He knew he wouldn't get the call-back for this interview. So, he hung up his jacket when he got home from it and said, "I've got to work on my appearance next time, so I can score the next interview." Sure enough. He got no call-back from the interview but simply a canned message from the company that said that his candidacy had been rejected.

CHAPTER 8

YOU'RE HERE! NOW WHAT?

Alright, let's get to it. You've done everything to prepare, showed up on time (preferably 10-15 minutes before your scheduled time of course) and it's show time, baby!

But remember this...

01. Your interview has already started...BE POLITE!

Do you know when your interview starts? Before you even enter the building. Aside from the possibility that the interviewer(s) have been checking you out online and on social media, the interviewers may also be checking you out on your way into the building. They may be looking out of the window to see if you pull in rushing or rudely cut someone off forms parking space. They may check with the lot attendant (of there is one), the security guard, or front desk staff.

02. Be polite! Show some manners!

I bet you've heard stories of someone cutting another person off in traffic or in the parking lot, only to find that that person will be the interviewer. It really happens! And that person at the interview desk you were pushy with and talked to in a condescending tone! Yes...they may be asked for their opinion of you! Don't lose the job opportunity before you ever even sit down!

03. Show that you're happy to be there!

It amazes me how I've seen some people await their interview time with frowning faces and seemingly-sulking body language. If you look like you don't want to be there, somebody just might think that you don't want to be there. And they won't want you there anymore either!

Sit with some poise and try to relax. They've invited you to learn more about you, and that's a great thing! So far they like you! Try to keep it that way.

When your name is called, try to get up and approach with energy and confidence.

Even if you're scared out of your mind, just remember that they're people too, people you might be working with one day. Give a good, strong handshake (web-to-web, firm but not crushing) and look the person in their eyes as you introduce yourself. Feel free to thank them now for taking the time to interview you.

04. Be yourself...your best, most polite, and engaging self! Be pleasant!

Follow the leader.

Most likely, you haven't been at this company before. Walk with but slightly behind so that you can follow without appearing to already take over. If they seem very quiet, it's fine to ask how their day is going (or even to make the common weather comment), but don't try to chat them up too much; some people are super annoyed by small talk.

If you're really nervous you can admit that (and

blame your excitement about this awesome opportunity), but don't make a big deal about it. If the interviewer is talking, listen carefully. You have the chance to learn something, whether about the person talking, the company, or the interview itself.

Remember: the interview has already started, so be mindful. This is NOT the time to share a lot of personal information, so pay attention of the person is "casually" asking questions about family and the like. They may be trying to soften you up so that they can learn more than you may normally be willing to share. I'm not telling you these things to scare you; I just want you to be aware of certain tactics that some (not all) interviewers use.

Once you're in the room, sit where you're directed. If you're not directed, ask where you should sit. It's easier than apologizing for sitting in someone's chair. How do you feel if someone comes to your house and just plops down before being invited?

A few bonus reminders...

Don't chew gum during your interview.

Don't interrupt.

Don't forget to introduce yourself; when you do, use their title and last name (e.g. Mr. Brown, Miss Curl) unless they tell you different.

Don't give a weak handshake.

Don't forget to turn off your cellphone ringer, including alarms.

Don't answer your cellphone or check messages, email, or social media during your interview.

CHAPTER 9

EFFECTIVELY NEGOTIATE YOUR SALARY

Believe it or not, salary negotiations begin immediately upon finding a position that interests you. One of the very first pieces of information you will notice is whether a company posts a salary range within their job description. Similarly, if a recruiter contacts you, he will either provide you with that information, or not, regardless of whether he is in possession of that information.

In either scenario, it is very important to understand that all legitimate open jobs at companies have pre-determined budgets tied to them. In other words, companies already know what they are willing to pay candidates for every new position.

Unfortunately, the majority of job descriptions do not contain the salary range and, while I wish it was a requirement to do so, companies have the right to keep this information hidden. However, this does not mean they also have the upper hand when it comes to negotiating the salary for the position.

That's why this chapter is so important. Even without knowing the salary, you are no longer at a disadvantage when it comes to negotiating a fair and reasonable compensation package for yourself.

Note: Every interaction you have will be unique. Some companies will start the salary discussion on the first interview while some will wait until later in the process. As a general rule, do not agree to a second, in-person interview until you have established the salary you are seeking is in-line with what the company is willing to pay. There is no point in going any further before knowing the new position will make sense for you financially.

The Question You Will No Longer Directly Answer

The way salary discussions used to work (and sadly, still do, in many cases) was job seekers began the negotiations by answering the following question from either recruiters or HR:

What is your current salary? -or- What were you making at your previous role?

Over time, this question has become so commonplace that very few job seekers question its relevance and, instead, willingly give up their personal information. The problem is that companies then take this information and use it as a starting point **for what they are going to offer you.**

Note: Some companies even have the audacity to request your old W-2 tax forms. Never hand these documents over.

As an example, let's assume a company has internally budgeted a hypothetical new job at $90K/year (and is not including a salary range in their job description) and you are currently making $75K. Additionally, this new position is absolutely the next logical step up for you from your current position.

Guess what's likely to happen if you divulge your current salary?

The company is going to offer you a little over what you are currently making (say $80K) so you get a salary increase but they save money.

But, isn't that fair?

No, that is not fair. The company/job seeker dynamic is a marketplace. There are buyers (companies) and there are sellers (job seekers) and the price is determined by supply and demand among other factors.

If a company is looking for a "Department Manager," for example, then, based on many market factors, which we'll discuss in a moment, there is a salary range that makes sense for that position.

A candidate's previous salary is not one of those factors.

As an exaggerated, but relevant, example to illustrate this point, imagine you bought a home 20 years ago for $200,000. In the present day, you know the house is now worth roughly $400,000 and you're looking to sell. What if a potential buyer offered you $225,000 since it's more than you paid? What would you do? You would tell them your home is worth about $400,000 based on the market and they need to get serious with their offer.

The exact same thing applies to your job salary.

Your current and past salaries are totally irrelevant for future positions.

The good news is that times are changing and diligent job seekers (like you) know that any personal salary questions asked of you from this point forward are off-limits and you will not answer them ever again.

In fact, these questions are now illegal in several locations (including Massachusetts, New York, California, Connecticut, among many other states and cities)4 and rightfully so. It's no one's business to know what your salary is except for you, your company, your accountant (if you have one), and anyone else with whom you choose to share your information. That's it. You wouldn't share this information with strangers. Don't share it with recruiters or companies.

Your New Approach

You will, instead, provide your salary range for a position based on your research of the position and your current situation. We will cover the research steps in a moment.

First, here is a conversation, based on an actual, initial phone discussion with a third-party recruiter, that best illustrates how to implement this approach. Keep in mind this discussion can be used with anyone, not only recruiters.

Story: In this example, a third-party recruiter initially posted a job title and a general, two sentence description of an open position online. Other topics were discussed during the call and then the salary topic came up.

Recruiter: So, what is your current compensation package?

Job seeker: I'm happy to provide my salary range for this position once you send me the description and we discuss the role in more detail.

Recruiter: I will, but I need to understand what you're making now.

Job seeker: I'm sorry but I'm not comfortable discussing that information.

Recruiter: [Silence] Can you, at least, give me an estimate? I just need it for a basis.

Job seeker: No, but I can give you a range of what I'm looking for once I know more about the role.

Recruiter: Okay. I ask everyone this question, but let's move on. What else do you need to know?

There are a couple of things to mention about this conversation that are very telling in only a few sentences.

1. She "needs" to understand what the Job Seeker is making now. Alternatively, you may get "the company needs to know..."

2.   This is total nonsense.

3.   They don't need to know that information. They want that information as it gives them tremendous leverage when it comes to negotiating your salary.

4.   An estimate for a "basis."

She's asking for your salary in a softer way. Don't fall for it. She wants a starting point to peg your next salary to. The salary that you are currently making in a different role at a different company has nothing to do with the role you are seeking and is, therefore, not a "basis" for anything.

What if a company or a recruiter says we can't continue the conversation without my current salary?

Then count your blessings they gave you a clear sign of what life is like at that company. If they don't value your financial privacy and don't think paying you a fair wage is important, then you don't need to work there. I can pretty much guarantee other aspects of that company are broken as well.

Move on and forget them.

A recruiter once told me my current salary will be revealed during a background check. Is this true?

Two things here:

1.	Your former company is only supposed to confirm your employment dates and the job titles you held. That's it. Your annual reviews and any other personal information should not be shared outside of the company. However, not everything is always in our control which is why...

2.	It doesn't matter. You have every right to be paid fairly and if the new company finds out you're getting a big "raise" with the salary you are asking for, then good for them. Again, if they are not willing to pay you fairly, then you don't need to work there. That kind of behavior is a strong sign about how a company operates. If they can't treat you well during the interview process, then there is a good chance there will be other issues once you're on board. Watch the signs!

Do the Research

Note: Some job listings may say something along the lines of "salary commensurate with experience." If you see language like that, it's the same as if the salary is not posted. That company doesn't want to tip their hand to job seekers and this, as you now know, doesn't matter.

If a salary is posted within the job description, all you need to do is ensure the range is in line with what you are seeking. Keep in mind that you must read the job description carefully to understand as much as you can about the role, including the location, before determining if the salary range posted is reasonable and meets your needs.

If there is no salary posted, then you will still apply and/or send in your résumé and a cover letter. Just realize that you'll need to take the steps I'm about to outline before you speak with anyone at the company. You need to be prepared to tell them exactly what you are looking for in terms of compensation.

There is so much valuable (and free) information available, including relevant salary details, that will allow you to come to the negotiating table prepared and ready to discuss a mutually agreeable salary range and eventual offer.

Start with helpful websites like Glassdoor, LinkedIn, and Salary.com. All three of those sites, among other insights, have a lot of information to help you get an understanding of what a typical salary range is for the position you are seeking in the relevant location.

Now, while you already know the salary range for the specific position you are considering will not be listed, you can easily find similar roles at similar companies in similar geographical areas.

This is the same thing home sellers do when assessing how high to list their house on the market. They look at the "comps"— comparable homes in the area. You're doing that here utilizing the job titles, job descriptions, and location. You will want to get five or six different salaries so you can confidently provide the company with a reasonable salary range.

Note: Geography is really important, especially if you're looking to relocate. Jobs in and around New York City or other major cities will typically pay more than smaller towns for similar roles simply because it costs you more to live and/or work in or around those large cities.

What to Look For

1.   Job title – Job titles are not standard and will vary among companies.

2.   Job responsibilities – Pay close attention to what your responsibilities will be versus what you are currently doing to confirm this new role is a step-up to more responsibilities (if that's what you're looking for) or not (if that's not what you're looking for). Additionally, make sure the position is something you want to do. Don't forget to also know how much travel will be required for the role.

3.   Geographic location – Is the position in or near a big city, a small city, or a more suburban area? What will your commute be like? What will your commute cost in terms of time and money?

4. Benefits – This includes health insurance, 401(k), vacation time, and other perks.

1. Note: You may not have all of the benefits information at first. That's okay. Assume there are benefits and if you find out different information later on, you can adjust your range. Companies need to be transparent with this information during the interview process and if they are not, you can certainly adjust your figures to meet your needs as well (i.e. a higher base salary if no health benefits are offered).

5. Alternative to your current situation / intangibles – Maybe you are currently unhappy at your job or maybe you're unemployed. Those two situations will impact you differently than if you are happily employed, casually exploring other potential opportunities out there. After you have all of the information (post-interviews), the last piece that goes into your decision has to do with all of the other factors that are unique to your life and current situation. We'll cover this topic later in the chapter.

Pretty straightforward, right? The key is to take the

extra time to dig into job descriptions a little more by utilizing available information so you come to the negotiation table fully prepared.

Next Step

Okay, so let's say you have established your desired salary range of $90-$95K works for the company and they also want to make you an offer.

If you're working with a third-party recruiter, you and she will typically hash out the details verbally and then the company will present you with a formal offer letter. If you're working directly with the company, the verbal back and forth may or may not happen and you may just be presented with a letter. Either way is fine. The offer letter is what counts.

The offer letter is where all of the details for your new position need to be stated. This includes, but is not limited to:

- Job title
- Start date
- Base salary

- Bonus potential

- Vacation time

- Name of your direct manager

- Benefits (health insurance, 401(k), etc.)

Note: There is typically a lot of legal language included with offer letters. Read it all very carefully and make sure you understand everything before you sign. If you have questions, contact the company and speak with someone until all of your questions are answered.

Wrapping Up

Receiving an offer is a great accomplishment and one that you should feel proud of. Let's take one last scenario and story to bring this chapter to a close.

If we continue with our previous example, let's say you receive an offer letter which states a base salary of $90K, three weeks' vacation, 15% potential bonus to be paid at the end of the year, full benefits, and reporting to Rob.

You have a choice here. The base salary is at the low end of your range, but you really liked Rob during your interview and you're excited that he will be your manager. The vacation time, which is actually a week more than you currently have, is secretly more important to you than any potential base salary increase the company may be willing to make. The rest of the terms are as expected.

CHAPTER 10

DON'T FORGET THE BODY LANGUAGE

First, body language is important because the employer will be reading your nonverbal cues. They will be listening to your words, but they will also be looking at how you are acting. Body language is something that everyone notices, so this is also true about your interviewer. They will notice if you are not making eye contact, and they will assume this is because you are nervous or not confident. They will also notice if you have a firm handshake, and they will believe you are confident and that you are successful through this. Because the interviewer is going to be noticing your body language, you should be noticing your own as well. If you are aware of your own body language, you can control it.

Let's talk about power body language. Power body language is a way to use your nonverbal communication to seem successful and confident. If you use body language that makes you appear confident, it will give you power in situations like interviews. Let's look into the components of power body language and the other body language tools you should use when you are in an interview.

First, make sure that you have a strong handshake. A strong handshake shows you are confident and successful. It shows you are not afraid of what is going to happen. Shake the interviewer's hand with a firm hand and a strong shake.

While you are shaking the interviewer's hand, introduce yourself, and make eye contact. Eye contact is important in your handshake, but it is also important for the rest of the interview at the same time. Eye contact is important because it shows you are both confident and interested. If you do not make eye contact, it can make you either seem like you are not interested in the job or it can make you seem like you are nervous. Both of these qualities are things that they are definitely not interested in. If you make eye contact, however, you seem interested and confident. These are qualities that people who are conducting interviews will see, and they will want. Eye contact is an easy thing to do, so it is something that you should always include in your interview skills.

You should also make sure that you are smiling. If you are smiling, it shows you were happy to be there. It shows you are friendly and that you are interested in the job. It shows you were happy to have the chance to interview for the job that you are seeking. It shows you are confident and you deserve to be there. It shows you are good enough and you believe it. If it might seem like you are not interested in the job or that you feel you do not deserve to be there. You do not want this to be the case, so make sure you keep a smile on your face.

Also, make sure that your body language is relaxed. Try to relax your jaw as this helps you relax the rest of your body. If you are relaxed, you will seem more confident and less nervous. Most employers want laid-back employees and not stressed ones. For this, if you seem relaxed, you will see more like the type of employee that they are looking for.

Make sure that you also sit and stand with your shoulders back. Sit up straight and keep the appropriate amount of distance in between you and then if you are. If you do this, you will seem like you are confident and that you are respectful towards the person interviewing you.

Other tools that can be helpful include active listening. Active listening includes eye-contact, nodding your head, smiling and letting the interviewer speak. It means you will never interrupt the interview while they are speaking. Typically, interviews are always about the applicant. This can be tiring for the person who is conducting the interview. If you show you are interested in what the interviewer says and that you care about them as a person, you can help them to feel better, and your interview in the process. The person who is conducting your interview is likely to remember this feeling.

Your body language can help you show you are interested in the job. Consider bringing a notebook and pen with you and taking notes on what you are saying. Also, you could include in this notebook a list of questions. When the interviewer gives you the answers to these questions, you could write the answers down in your notebook. This shows you are serious, and it shows you are prepared. It shows you care enough about the job to bring notes home to read later. This is also a step that most people do not take the time or effort to do. For this, it can make you stand out from the crowd. I can make the interviewer remember you long after the interview has taken place.

As you can see, there are many things to remember when you are in an interview. When you get to an interview, the person who is interviewing you liked your application so much that they wanted to meet you in person. This will likely give you a boost of confidence because you already know that you were set apart in a small group of successful applicants. It means your application was considered better than many others. Interviews can be nerve-racking but think of them as a way to make a great first impression. You already made a great first impression on paper; you just need to do it in person now.

CHAPTER 11

COMMON PITFALLS AND HOW TO DEAL WITH THEM

Everyone knows climbing the world's largest mountain requires an expert guide. And if you have an imperfect resume, you have a big mountain to climb as you try to reach your career summit. I can be your expert guide because I, too, have had an imperfect resume: I come across on paper as a job hopper. Over my career, I've made many attempts to climb my Career Mount Everest, despite my imperfect resume, and I have learned the critical lessons needed for success. At this point in my career, I have worked for almost ten different companies and in two different countries, the U.S. and Australia. Each career move was a calculated career move to acquire new skills and experiences. Unfortunately, this strategy, while advancing my skill set, has at times flagged me as a job hopper.

From experience, the job search process is at least twice as difficult and requires more effort if you don't have a perfect resume. Blemishes such as long gaps, a high volume of jobs, and/or legal issues are just a few red flags that often scare off potential employers. Don't be completely discouraged though if your resume is less than perfect; you can overcome this challenge.

Recently, I found inspiration in a fortune cookie: "life is more difficult near the summit." This quote can have a positive impact on your mindset. Think of your current status of your dream job search process as if you are climbing a mountain. Some of you may feel as if you are climbing Mount Everest. Take a moment to pause and reflect on the significant progress you have made. You may not realize how very close you are to achieving your ultimate goal. The summit is right before you. To reach the peak though, you need additional perseverance and some timely insider secrets.

Through facing these challenges, I learned to overcome my resume's imperfections. You too can overcome blemishes on your record or experience based on past mistakes or gaps in your resume. If you are attempting to make a career change, you can do it even if your previous experience and education doesn't perfectly align with the roles that you're seeking out.

Dealing With Blemishes On Your Record Or Experience

You can address these issues in your cover letter. Additionally, consider bringing it up in the interview first before the interviewer asks. This is an advanced negotiation skill where you are in control of how this information is presented. By addressing the elephant in the room, you disarm any personal reservations you subconsciously hold. Alternatively, it could be something the interviewer has in the back of his or her mind, and unless you address it, he or she may not be able to get over it.

The best advice in all your communications is to be honest and transparent. Explain the situation. If you made a mistake, explain you made a mistake, but you learned from it. That's the point that you want to spend more time on. Go into more details on the lessons you learned. What do you know now that you wish you would have back then? You want to keep the focus on establishing that you're a different person now and you've taken steps to improve yourself. You should explicitly guarantee that those same mistakes won't happen again. These responses will help your prospective employer overcome their initial reservations.

Please take the time before you start any job search process to remove any self-created blemishes. By that, you should perform an external, unbiased review of all your social media accounts—Facebook, LinkedIn, Twitter, Instagram—and delete posts and pictures that would create some unnecessary questions about your character. Depending on the severity of your posts, pictures, and overall profile, it may be best if you delete the profile in its entirety. It is all right to start a new profile or account to prevent any misconceptions that a prospective employer would hold against causing him or her to pass your resume by. As a tip to ensure you stay proactive in managing your social media presence, do not press send without asking "Would I be comfortable with this being shown on the cover of the Wall Street Journal? Or being sent directly to my boss or client?" If not, delete it.

Overcome Employment Gaps

Generally speaking, employment gaps of one or two months are normal and expected. Most recruiters and hiring managers will not identify this length of gap in work experience as an issue. However, if you have a gap that is three months or longer, you will need to spend more time crafting interview responses that provide more details concerning your extended break in employment. Make sure your explanations are credible and thorough to address the interviewers concerns.

You should take the same approach when dealing with resume blemishes: explain it in your cover letter and address it during the interview. You want to explain the situation that caused you to end your previous employment. Do provide enough details so the interviewer has no objection to hiring you. In the event you were terminated, share your lessons learned and how those experiences will help you in the job you are interviewing for. Be prepared as there is a high probability everyone you interview with will ask you about it. You want to make sure you have your story memorized, and you are clear and confident in your responses.

How To Make A Career Change

You may have gone to school, graduated, and pursued a career that someone recommended or you thought would be the right fit for you. Unfortunately, after a few years working in that industry, it just was not resonating with your passion. If you find yourself in this situation, it's going to be a bit more of a challenge for you to get past the initial rounds in the interview process. To be successful in your job search, you will have to rely more heavily on your network if you don't want to start over at entry level positions. You should also volunteer for organizations that can help you develop experiences and transferable skills— communication, cultural awareness, change management etc.—which will help you be successful in a new career.

If you can obtain these important skills, then your chances of success increase dramatically. Possessing these valuable skills may help a prospective employer overlook any other skills or experience gap you may have.

So rest assured, you can overcome the imperfect resume; it is all about open, honest communication; addressing it first yourself; and gaining valuable skills which help you shine despite any resume flaws.

CONCLUSION

As we wind up this guide, it is important to know that there are competitive advantages of working for Amazon. The major competitive advantages that Amazon has are the household name and its customer retention. As one of the companies that brought e-commerce to the forefront, customers trust the company and regularly choose their site to buy from. This trust and massive customer base is one of the strongest advantages of Amazon.

Strengths

Strong Foundation and Finances: While Amazon was initially built on books, their product categories have expanded to include almost anything that can be found commercially available today, making them one of the biggest companies in the business.

Client-focused: Their long existence has also allowed them to develop tools that allow them to tailor-fit offers and advertising based on preferences drawn from the buying behavior of their clients. As over half of their clients become repeat customers, there is a low cost of acquisition of new clients.

Price Leader: Due to its long background in the business, Amazon has been able to develop advantageous alliances with other companies, especially those specializing in logistics. This allows them to make use of the principles of economies of scale, allowing for lower prices and more efficient inventory replenishment, minimizing losses. They have also built a delivery infrastructure that ensures quick, cheap, and reliable delivery of their products, even to the more remote regions.

Global Perspective: Amazon has a practice of maintaining local ties on a global scale, meaning that in each country they operate in, they partner with local businesses and tailor their branding to fit to the local environment. They call it "Going global and acting local".

Weaknesses

Lower Margins: Amazon's profit margins have been shrinking due to price wars **with**

competitors.

Tax avoidance: Amazon's efforts to reduce their taxes have resulted in negative publicity, especially in the United States and United Kingdom, both major markets **for the company.**

Debt: In smaller countries with smaller markets, Amazon is still not turning a profit, and all the while has been accumulating debt.

Flops: Certain Amazon products did not launch as strongly as they wanted them to, such as the Fire Phone, and the Kindle Fire.

Composition of Management

One of the key figures of the Amazon team is one of the founders and the CEO of the company, Jeff Bezos. It would serve any prospective applicant well to conduct research on Bezos, along with his management and operational principles.

Basic Metrics and Company Financial Data

Since the numbers tend to change rapidly, it's highly

recommended to research on this as close to possible to your interview. Amazon often runs at a loss, but their growth continues to move upwards. As of the most recent data at the time of writing, Amazon's customer base is around three hundred million (300,000,000).

Future Plans of the Company and Possible Threats

As always, researching on your own would be best, but here are some possible plans and threats to the company that may be useful to keep in mind when you head to the interview.

Possible Plans:

Product integration: Similar to Kindle and other attempts, perhaps Amazon can begin producing their own products in certain categories and developing their brand through various product lines.

Strategic Expansion: Targeting countries with untapped markets and low saturation, such as developing Asian countries may allow for rapid expansion.

Targeted acquisition: Amazon can use its clout to acquire smaller e-commerce companies, allowing them to decrease the competition while improving certain specialized services and products. They can also open a physical store in select locations, allowing for better brand engagement.

Possible Threats:

Low Barriers to Entry: By its nature, e-commerce has a relatively low barrier to entry, allowing for more players in the market, leading to price wars that cut into profit margins.

Regulations: Un-updated government regulation, especially on matters of Foreign Direct Investments has slowed down growth in certain areas, especially the developing world.

Local Competition: Though Amazon tries to integrate locally, homegrown sites and services can prove to be difficult competitors, such as SnapDeal in India.

The Company in the News

This part is quite simple, as you can always flip to the business section of the newspaper or run a quick search on Google. Perhaps there may have been a recent acquisition or expansion, or maybe a slowdown in growth. It would be best to keep updated on news, even reading in the morning of the day of your interview, so you can demonstrate how prepared you are to the interviewer.

All the best!

Made in the USA
San Bernardino, CA
15 December 2019

61534879R00104